Augusta "Ada" King, Countess of Lovelace, is often called the first computer programmer. This is incredible, as when she was born in 1815, there were no computers, and no schools or universities where girls could study.

Ada's mother, Annabella Milbanke, however, was determined her daughter would be well-educated and would study maths and science, as well as stitching, singing, painting, and running a house.

Ada's father was the poet Lord Byron. Her mother and father had separated shortly after she was born, and Ada lived with her grandmother for some of her childhood. Her father left the country a month after she was born and never returned. So Ada never saw her father.

When Ada was growing up she had a number of illnesses, including measles. Ada's illnesses meant that she had to rest much of the time, and she spent a lot of this time quietly studying.

In 1835, when she was just 19 (nineteen), Ada married the man who was to become the Earl of Lovelace. This meant that she would become the Countess of Lovelace, and that is why she is known as Ada Lovelace.

Earl of Lovelace

Ada was always interested in mechanical things. As a child, she had drawn fancy boats and steam-powered planes. Ada's mother encouraged her interest in maths, and found extremely good teachers for her.

One of those teachers was Mary Somerville. Mary was an incredibly intelligent lady and studied maths and astronomy.

Mary Somerville introduced Ada to Charles Babbage. Charles Babbage is often called 'the father of the computer'. He was building a "Difference Engine", which was a tower of numbered wheels. When a handle was turned it could calculate sums. Having seen it, aged 17 (seventeen), Ada had started to write to Babbage about what he was doing.

Before calculators or computers were invented it took a long time to solve complex sums. A person had to do the maths problems. They used mathematical tables or charts to help speed the process up.

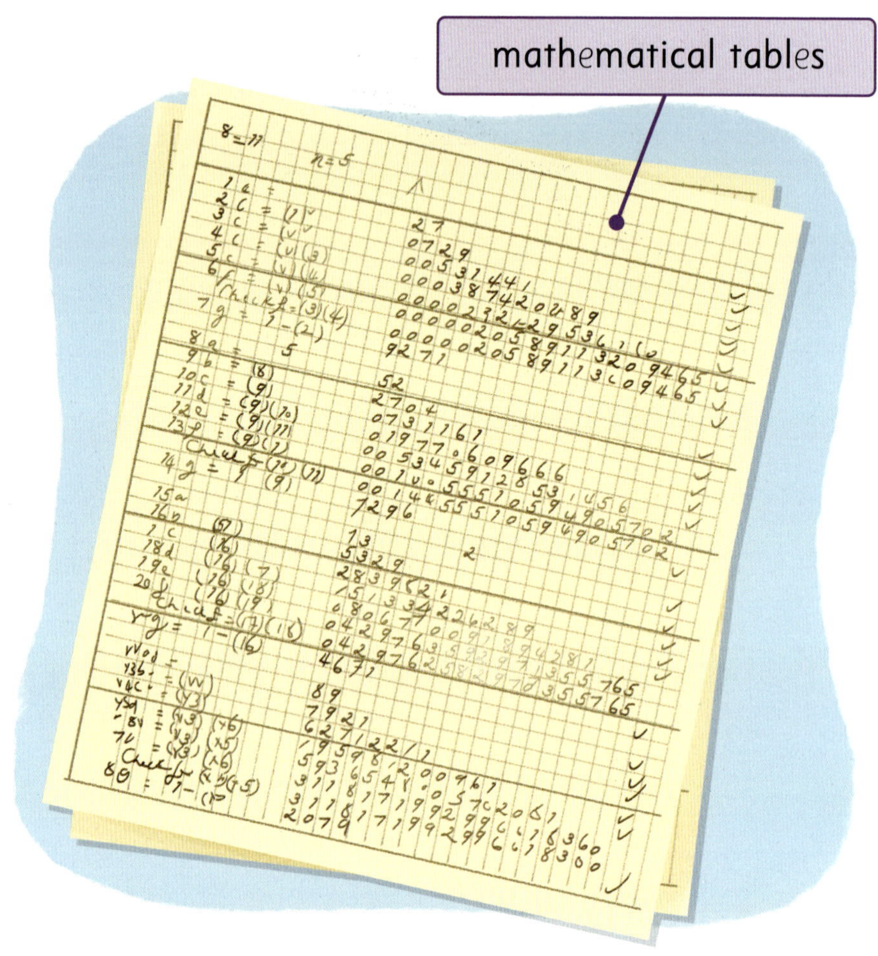

The mathematical tables were written out by people who were called “computers”. This is where the name “computers” comes from!

One of Charles Babbage's jobs was to check numbers on mathematical tables. He decided to build a calculating device to do the job for him.

Charles Babbage planned to build another engine. It used cards with holes punched in them to programme it. He copied the idea from the Jacquard Loom, which used cards with holes in them to produce patterns on woven fabric.

Babbage's idea was that instead of just putting in the sum and getting the result, the engine could pause at certain points and then choose from one of two different ways to continue. This meant it would be able to complete far more complex sums.

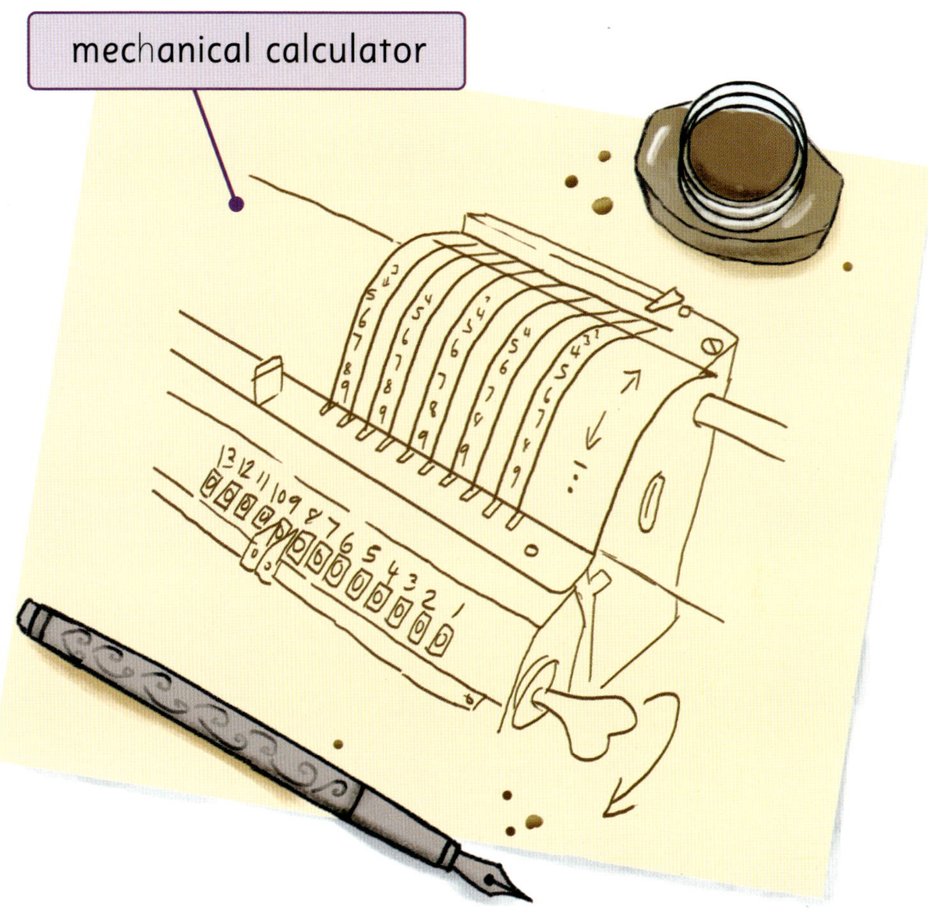

The holes of the punched cards would instruct the mechanical calculator.

Charles Babbage's engines were not considered very interesting by most scientists at the time, and Babbage never got to make them.

An Italian called Menabrea agreed to look at Babbage's ideas and write about them. He wrote a report of about 8,000 (eight thousand) words in French, which was published in a Swiss journal.

Ada agreed to translate this report but, importantly, she also added some notes of her own. Ada's report was about 20,000 (twenty thousand) words long – three times the length of the original report.

In one of the notes she produced the first published step-by-step sequence of how to solve certain mathematical problems.

It is because of the step-by-step sequence Ada wrote that she is regarded as the first computer programmer.

Sadly, as Babbage's mechanical calculator engine was not built, the programme was not used at the time. The first Babbage engine to be built was actually completed in the year 2002 - 153 years later.

Ada was the first person to think that devices could do more than just find the answers to mathematical problems. She argued that music or pictures could be translated into numbers and used by computers. This was amazing as no one else had ever imagined that computers could do this.

The importance of what Ada wrote was not recognized, however, until many years later. It has been suggested that Ada's notes inspired a man called Alan Turing.

Alan Turing was a codebreaker in World War 2, who solved the very complex codes that the Germans used to send secret messages. To do this, Turing and his team built computers using Ada's notes and concepts.

Incredibly, over 100 (one hundred) years later, Ada's cleverness was recognized. The computer language "Ada," created for the American Defence Department, was named after her.

From November 2015, all new British passports have Ada's and Charles Babbage's images on one of the pages.